Explore
Every Day

365 Daily Prompts to Refresh Your Life

INTRODUCTION

Hey, we get it: travel is great. Seeing the world with new eyes, eating new foods, meeting people from different cultures. We learn, we explore, we challenge ourselves. We return all the better for having refreshed and renewed our outlook.

And we always say the same thing: 'I really should do more of this at home. No, really, this time, I swear. I could go to more local museums or visit new neighbourhoods or get out into nature.'

And then, we don't.

There are actually scientific reasons why we don't. So, for now, don't beat yourself up about it. We get it. I mean, we're Lonely Planet, and we're as guilty as anyone. Who has the time for wild adventures after a long day at work? Have you seen that pile of dust under the sofa? Our to-do lists seem to have grown tentacles as they pull us down towards productivity and day-to-day survival.

So think of this book not as a simple guide to fun things to do, but as an act of rebellion. As a stand against the forces that hold us back from exploring our creativity, our adventurousness and our communities. You don't need to fly to the Maldives and stay in an above-water bungalow or trek through the Himalayas for months on end to awaken that sense of adventure or connection.

You have no excuse, either. Some of these prompts take an actual, literal minute (breathe deeply; p6), others a full day or more (living-room camping; p90) but most take anywhere between 10 minutes to an hour. The vast majority of them are completely or almost free.

These 365 prompts (plus one leap prompt, of course) offer a dozen different types of archetypal experiences. Do you want to connect with family (call a relative; p86), friends (hide a note for a mate; p158) or your community (use your volunteer skills; p156)? Do you want to appreciate art (mural walking tour; p13) or would you rather create something yourself (draw a map of your town; p10)? You can editorialise your home town (a travel-writing assignment; p35) or just use your imagination (dedicate today to your favourite person in history; p112). And yes, you can even recast your housework as fun (turn a chore into a game; p64).

But if you promise not to tell your brain, we'll share the real scientific secret: counter-intuitively, adding breaks to your daily life will help you become more productive. In fact, these mini-breaks can be more beneficial than long trips. Einstein was famous for what he called combinatory play; in fact, he credited violin breaks as the catalyst to much of his best work. 'Combinatory play seems to be the essential feature in productive thought,' he said.

You might notice the prompts are almost entirely interactive, or at least involve taking steps to prepare you for action. When we think back to what gave us that spark of joy during the day, was it that time you spent on social media or reading the news? Or was it the dusty orange sunset you saw on the way home, or that conversation you had with a new colleague? We can't take away the former (well, we do try: unfollow one social media account, p78; and don't read any news today, p36) but this book will help remind you to do more of the latter.

Sometimes creativity and exploration require baby steps and we've got you covered there too. Several prompts are two- or four-parters and many have extra credit. What have you always wanted to do that frightens you (research something that scares you; p50)? Find out where you could do it nearby then sleep on it for a day. Or a week. Or a month. It doesn't matter; simply doing the research totally counts as one complete prompt. You get a gold star! If you're inspired to share, you could pass on the prompt (ask about an adventurous thing; p40) to a friend, relative or even a child in the family, and help them add more exploration and adventure to their lives. They'll soon become seasoned travellers, at home and away.

BY ALEX LEVITON

Admire the next piece of street art or graffiti you see as if it were hanging in an art gallery.

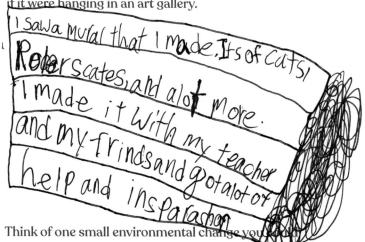

I saw a mural that I made, Its of cats! Roler scates, and alot more. I made it with my teacher and my frinds and got alot of help and insparashen

Think of one small environmental change you could make and act on it.

Buy a fruit or vegetable you've never eaten before.

Quick: name the first country that comes to mind.
Find a film from that country and watch it.
Write the review here:

Ascend to the highest point in your town (buildings count).

Learn a word from your region's indigenous culture or some local slang.

Breathe in for four seconds. Exhale for six.

Spend one full minute really, truly feeling the weather.

(1/4) Empires were built – and destroyed – over the search for aromatic spices. Research where in your town you can find dozens available instantly (health-food and international stores often have large spice sections).

(2/4) Give yourself a full 10-15 minutes to browse through and deeply inhale as many spices and herbs as you can.

(3/4) Choose one that tickles your fancy yet is totally unfamiliar to you and buy it (saving you the 200-year-long journey to attain it).

(4/4) Find a recipe that incorporates the new spice and cook it.

Draw
A MAP
of your town

Extra credit
Find a willing partner, give yourselves three minutes each to draw,
then compare results afterwards. What stood out for each of you?

Get dressed up and conduct a photo shoot with a friend.

Many world-famous universities (UC Berkeley, Cambridge, the Sorbonne) offer free courses online. Sign up to one and learn Shakespeare, Roman history or opera.

Which neighbourhood in your town is most different to your own? Spend an afternoon running errands there.

Go on a mural walking tour.
Describe your favourite:

Find a tree or plant in your neighbourhood and give it a nickname based on its personality.

Write down a favourite quote and place it somewhere you'll see it every day for a week.

Look around the room you're in and describe something
that makes you happy:

Find someone to partner with for this book. For the next
week or month, pick a prompt to do each day and then
share your experiences.

Make an object out of household items: a lava lamp, vinegar cleaning spray or seashell wind chimes, perhaps.

You know that big trip you've always wanted to do? Pick a future date (ie, India, 11–25 February six years from now) and start reading about it, planning and saving for it.

Attend a storytelling event. Extra credit: sign up to tell a story yourself.

Go on an international holiday near your house: stay at a nearby youth hostel or shared guesthouse that's popular with travellers. Cook a meal and start a chat.

Find an object in the middle distance. Focus on it, and only it, for one whole minute. If your attention wanders, gently bring it back.

Place two slices of cucumber over your eyes and relax for five minutes.

Look out for unusual sign typography.
Recreate your favourite here:

Dress up at work today. Wear your most rock-star jacket or a tuxedo pocket square. Extra credit: add 1% of that character to your personality all day.

Visit a different religious place of worship in your own town. Extra credit: stay for coffee or social time afterwards and start up a conversation.

Find a nearby geocache. Get geocaching.

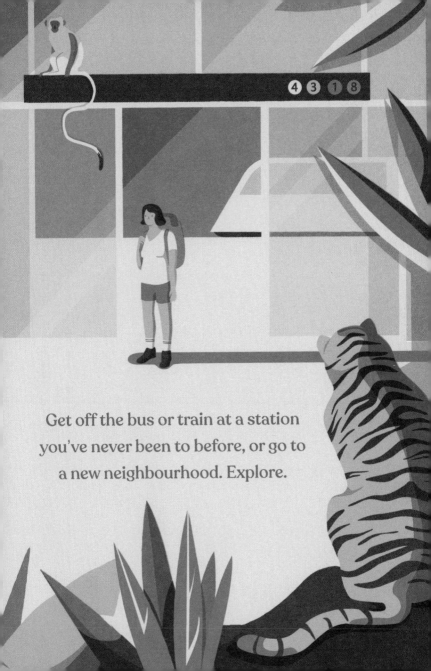

Get off the bus or train at a station you've never been to before, or go to a new neighbourhood. Explore.

Type the name of your town or a nearby city + an activity you've been meaning to try (Shanghai + ballroom dancing, Brussels + motocross racing, etc) into a search engine. Pick something from the first two pages of results and do it.

Draw a stick figure self-portrait:

(1/2) If you don't have a library card, stop in at your local library and get one. It will come in handy for this book.

(2/2) If you do have a library card, next time you go, pay off a stranger's overdue fines anonymously.

Look around you right now. Write down everything you see that begins with the letter P.

Name three things you're grateful for today.

What play or musical is your local community or student theatre company performing? Buy a ticket and go.

Seek out some flowers – whether outside or in a shop. Take the time to smell them.

In your next email or text of at least a few sentences, don't use the letter 'e'.

If your voicemail greeting has been the same for a while, change it.

Why do you travel? Circle all the words or phrases that apply. (Extra credit: add some words of your own.)

CULTURE   APPRECIATION   WELLNESS   BRAGGING RIGHTS

NATURE   PLAY   FOOD AND DRINK   CHALLENGE   PAMPERING

FUN   ADVENTURE   KNOWLEDGE   RELAXATION

ART AND MUSIC   CONNECTION   PERSPECTIVE   VOLUNTOURISM

INTROSPECTION   NEW EXPERIENCES   GELATO

Play 20 questions.

Borrow a dog
and take
it for a walk.

Dog owners: borrow a friend and take
them on your dog walk.

Book a table for tonight at a restaurant in
a neighbouring city.

Take a different route to work.

Choose a local amateur sports team to support and
go to watch them play.

Create flip-art animation with a stack of post-it notes.

Eat a dessert for breakfast and a breakfast dish for dinner.

Eat something you've picked yourself.

Find something nearby that's man-made (a building, perhaps, or a book or a road sign). Consider this: how did it come into existence? How many men and women were involved? Why was it made?

There are some 6000 mazes in 80 countries around the world. Find one near you and walk it.

Hug someone.

Describe your goal in exactly six words:

Leave a book you love on a bus or train for someone else to find and enjoy.

Look through the periodic table; what's your favourite element? Why?

One evening, turn off all electronics and screens at 6pm.
Read, talk or play games by candlelight until you go to sleep.

Whenever you run into that one person, you both keep
saying you really need to get together. Make the first move.

Open the entertainment section of your local newspaper. Close your eyes and point. Go to see whatever your finger lands on.

Eat something on a stick.

You've just been hired as a travel writer and your first assignment is to write 150 words about your hometown. Deadline is in one hour:

Don't read a single piece of news all day.

Sit outside with a notebook. Write down everything you see, hear, smell and sense for an hour straight.

Pick up one piece of rubbish and throw it away.

Follow an ant or other insect on its journey and make up a story about the richness of its inner life. Is it carrying a leaf that'll become a guest bed? Does the spider on your wall want to become a mime artist? Write your story here:

Wake up early
to listen to the
dawn chorus in
a local park or
woodland.

Sign up for a walking tour of your town or the nearest city, be it a history lesson, architecture tour, pub crawl or food tasting.

The Earth is rotating at 460m per second (about 1000 miles an hour). Spend one full minute trying to feel it.

Up your public-transport use one level. Take a bus somewhere for the very first time or find a route between two places you've never been and ride it.

Your top-secret mission today: think of an undisclosed word and subtly try to get someone to say it. (Some suggestions: candlestick; authority; trailblazing.)

Ask a friend or relative what adventurous or challenging thing they've always wished they could do. Help them do it.

Imagine that, at midnight, all shades of the colour green will morph into a sallow, lifeless grey. Spend today looking at the world with this in mind.

Pick up a cookbook at home or from the library (or find a cooking blog). Open it at page 63 (or its equivalent). Make that recipe.

Smile at exactly half of the people you see on the street. What did you notice?

Right this very second, close your eyes, breathe-in deeply and meditate for seven seconds.

Attend a government or public meeting. They're often livelier than you'd expect.

Shine on the outside; wear the brightest clothes you own.

Is someone sitting near you right now? Ask them to join you in a quick game of hangman, noughts and crosses or scissors, paper, stone.

If you were about to be sent back in time to one historic era, which would it be and why? Which one would you most definitely not choose?

Are you alone? Go ahead, make a weird sound.

Find a piece of art at a museum, gallery or even a café.

Spend 10 minutes focusing on it.

(3/4) What feelings does it evoke?

(4/4) What do you think the artist was feeling or wanted to get across? What strikes you the most about it?

Make a Random Acts of Kindness Day
pact with three friends. At the end of the
day, share your stories.

Think of something you've been meaning to do/always wanted to do that scares you.

Why does it scare you?

(3/4) Which five small steps could you take to pursue said activity?

(4/4) Choose the easiest. Draft your first step here:

Learn one new constellation

Which situation or conflict around the world would you like to know more about? Spend one hour familiarising yourself with its context. Find – and read – one person's story within that conflict.

Attend a free lecture at your nearest university.

Ask friends, family or social media to list five ingredients. Pick three and make a dish.

Fill a 'zombie box' with items you might need during a zombie attack (hiking shoes, snacks, spare money). If no zombies attack, feel free to keep the box packed and ready for spontaneous adventures.

What's the oldest structure in your town? Go see it.

Research where you could ride a horse near you.
Then make sure you actually go there and ride a horse.

Find the nearest restaurant or shop to you that sells edible insects. Eat one.

What's your favourite shape? Find items around you which are that shape and tell them you appreciate their triangleness or roundness.

Find a set of swings – and
swing. Extra credit: swing
until your toes touch the sky.

Look at the night sky as if you were a famous artist.

Write a fan letter to your favourite scientist, author or a former teacher.

Check your passport's expiry date.

At home, type 'museum' into an online map or GPS. See what quirky, fascinating or unusual places pop up near you. Pick one, and go.

Find out where you can listen to adventurers and adventure talks locally and go get inspired.

Stand up for a cause by performing one tangible action.

Rearrange your furniture. If absolutely everything is in its perfect place, move something just one centimetre or inch.

Watch the sunrise or sunset. Sketch or describe it here:

When you've got some time and you're ready to listen, ask someone, 'No, how are you *really*?'

Practise literomancy (fortune-telling using letters and words). Open a book and point at a word or sentence. What's it trying to tell you?

(1/4) Go to your local library. If you don't yet have a library card, get one. (See page 23).

(2/4) Delve through the shelves of row #1 until you find a fascinating book you'd normally never read. Check it out.

Next time you're at the library, go to row #2 and do the same thing.

Then row #3, row #4 and so on until you've gone through the entire library.

Some geneticists believe that everyone in the world is no more than 50th cousins removed. Keep it in mind as you go about your day.

Turn a chore into a game – how fast can two people put away dishes? What does mop-dancing look like?

If you could learn to do anything at all, what would it be? Spend 10 minutes researching how you might go about it.

Listen to a piece of classical music while conducting the entire time.

Your mission today: find something fluffy.
Extra credit: pet it (even if it's a coat).

Take home-cooked food to work to share with colleagues.

This week, make it a point to meet a neighbour.

Scientists have discovered that every advanced life form on Earth requires play. How can you add five minutes of play time to your day today?

Write a review of your favourite book or product.

Find an atlas or globe.
Spin it or point to a
random page. Wherever
you pick, start planning
your journey. If you land
on the middle of the ocean,
start planning your voyage.

Celebrate the season with a ritual. In spring, for instance, press a wildflower; in autumn, collect leaves; in winter, curl up inside with a good book.

What would be the very best thing about being five years old again? If there's a five-year-old in your family, ask them what they like most about it.

Think of an everyday item that tickles you. Postboxes? Stop signs? Go on a stop-sign or postbox tour of your town.

Today, wear an invisible cape that has the power to reflect everything negative.

Buy yourself a bouquet of flowers and rearrange them in your own style.

Find a slide and slide down it.

Create a 'blackout poem'. Find a novel or book and photocopy a page. Using a marker pen, black out words you don't want in your poem. What's left is your poem. Write that out here:

Go to an international food store. Ask the proprietor for suggestions and create a meal.

Pick a leaf and feel its textures and crevices. Notice its colours and shape. Write 150 words describing your leaf:

(1/2) Get a guidebook for your city or region and circle 12 new places you'd like to visit. Commit yourself to trying one place every month.

(2/2) Create your own list of 52 places in your town, one for every week of the year, where you could take visitors.

Go somewhere you know but you're not overly familiar with. What have you missed seeing before? Write it down here:

Eat your favourite food item as if it were for the last time.

Pick a body part – your left eyebrow, your forehead, your right hip – and lead with that all day.

Download a plant-recognising app or get a botany book from the library. Upload or look up three plants or flowers you've never been able to name.

List three things that made you smile today:

The next time you need customer service, ask the representative what the best part of their day was.

From what point in your town can you see the furthest? Go there and look as far as you can.

Buy a small amount of fish/bird/duck food and go feed some fish/birds/ducks.

What's one of your favourite smells? Grapefruit? Incense? Pine? Buy it (or the essential oil) and breathe in that smell all day.

You know that one social media account that makes you feel bad/sad/mad? Unfollow it.

What would you never do alone in your own town that you would do when travelling? Go to a comedy show? A restaurant? Do it this week at home.

Find a tourist. Ask them what type of things they like to do and give them great advice about where to do it.

Leave your postman or postwoman a thank-you note on your letterbox.

Sketch a local landmark:

Turn off all the lights in your house except for one and make shadow puppets. Extra credit: find someone and create a shadow-puppet story together.

Make it a point to be bored today. For one whole hour, if possible.

A surprising number of police forces have ride-along schemes. Ask your local force if you can participate.

(1/2) What's your lucky item? A coin, teddy bear, piece of jewellery, amulet?

(2/2) Take your lucky item with you to work today.
(Even if it's the teddy bear.)

What sound is the colour red? What about gold? White?

Get your hands dirty: feel the earth, dig up a weed, clean your car engine. Extra credit: make an honest-to-goodness mud pie.

Is there anything you want to start collecting on your travels? Begin by obtaining one from your own town.

Think of a style of music that intrigues you. Research it for 10 minutes.

If your house was on fire, what would you do? Physically enact your escape.

When you were a toddler, what did you always want to do? Eat biscuits for dinner? Stay up all night? Do it now, but on behalf of your younger self.

You know that one tech problem you keep having? Teach yourself how to solve it.

What is it that your town is known for making? Visit its source: a factory or farm tour, a cooking demonstration, a museum, etc.

Visit a cheese shop and taste three varieties you've never tried before.

Call an older relative to say hi.

Ask them to tell you a story about your family history.

(3/4) Ask them about a childhood memory that includes food.

(4/4) Ask them for a family recipe. Extra credit: write down the recipe for the whole family to enjoy.

Go to your region's history museum or website and learn one new fact about your area.

Read the news today, but from another country's perspective.

That wine or food item you've had in your cupboard forever? Open it tonight.

Go online and do a search for 'poetry' + an experience or emotion you've had. (For instance, 'poetry' + 'curious' or 'poem' + 'dinner'.) Click on one result and read it.

Memorise a joke today. Extra credit: tell it.

Silently give someone an award today: most polite, most collaborative co-worker, biggest smile on the bus, etc.

Set up a tent in your living room
(or your back garden) as if you
were camping out.

Extra credit: tell ghost stories or toast
marshmallows over the burner.

You know that weird statue in your town? Visit it and read about its history.

Suggest a sleepover to a friend. Stay up late, eat pizza, play games.

Sign up for a class.

Grab a piece of food – an almond, a raisin, chocolate
– and savour that and only that for a full five minutes.
Extra credit: describe it here:

Go to a bead shop and make a piece of jewellery.

Style your hair differently today. If you don't have any, draw a dot on your head and see if anyone notices.

Teach yourself how to fold an origami crane from the nearest piece of scrap paper.

Look around. What object in your house could you destroy? A magazine? Food packaging? Turn that object into an art project. Or simply destroy it, with no questions asked.

Buy chalk and make street art. Extra credit: create a drawing party.

Don't use your dominant hand for one hour.

Sing out loud in the bath or shower today.

Baking soda is ridiculously useful. Discover one new way to use it.

Join an urban scavenger hunt near you. Extra credit: if you can't find one, create one. Fact-finding scavenger hunts work great, by the way.

Visit the oldest cemetery near you. Which headstones fascinate you?

What cuisine have you never tried?
Ukrainian? Vegan? Malaysian?
Ethiopian? Visit a restaurant near
you that serves it.

1

Stretch out your next meal for as long as possible.
Two hours at a restaurant? A four-hour dinner party?

Which house or building in your town is your favourite?
Research the style, colours or architecture that makes it
your favourite.

Eat your meal with chopsticks if you usually use a fork.
If you usually use chopsticks, switch to a fork.

Think of what you love most about staying home and not
travelling. Write it here:

That one **touristy thing** in your region you've never done? Finally do it.

Ask a friend to introduce you to someone new.

Make a resolution, but one you only need to stick to for 30 days.

Read a book from another culture.

Pick up two small, non-breakable items and give juggling a go. Extra credit: go for the full three.

Go to a networking event.

Find a one-day volunteer opportunity.

Cosplay in the tiniest way possible today.

Attend a reading at your favourite book shop this week, no matter what book it is.

Watch a movie with subtitles in a language that you'd like to learn.

(1/2) Say yes to something you've always wanted to say yes to.

(2/2) Say no to something you've always wanted to say no to.

The next conversation you have, listen with so much attention you could answer a quiz about it afterwards.

Is there a theme restaurant near you? Maybe one with animatronic animals, costumes or singing? Go, but with the mindset that it's the greatest place on Earth.

Make the fanciest mocktail or cocktail from whatever you find in your kitchen. Extra credit: cut out and colour a little paper umbrella.

Do you eat or cook almost the same thing every day? Substitute one part of it.

Spot a bird and follow it for as long as you can.

Take photos of everything yellow you see today. Make a collage.

Think of someone you know who's going through a difficult situation. What small favour might they appreciate?

Skip. Literally: physically skip.

(1/4) Travel is all about a lack of routines, but what's one of your favourite routines? Why?

(2/4) And what's one of your least favourite routines?

(3/4) What's a routine you'd like to add to your day?

(4/4) Do your morning routine in an entirely different order.

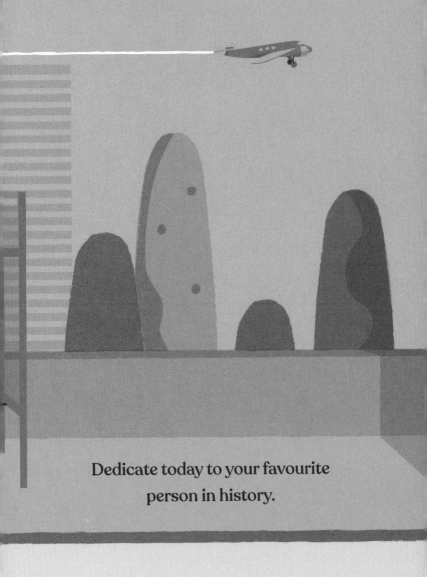

Dedicate today to your favourite person in history.

Visit a local botanical garden or arboretum and read the placards.

Search your region's tourism website for a new event or activity to try.

Do some genealogical research on your family until you find one new piece of information.

Locate the nearest trail to your house that you haven't been on and walk it (or hike, bike, rollerblade, etc).

On your next day outing, wake up ridiculously early or stay out outlandishly late (whichever feels more like a holiday).

Stop by your local fire or police station and bring them flowers or just offer them your thanks.

Donate an item you don't use any more to a charity.

Stare out of the nearest window. Sketch what you see:

Pay someone a deserved compliment.

Find one social media account from another country you want to visit, and follow it.

Pour milk into tea or coffee and watch the patterns. Describe them here:

Make up your own special holiday today. Extra credit: celebrate it every year on this date.

Write a haiku.

Shake your whole body for one minute. Extra credit: shake until you get the kinks out.

Wear a piece of clothing or jewellery you got while travelling.

Clean out your refrigerator or food cupboards.

Arrange a video chat with a group of your friends or family.

What places are twinned with your town?

Research them.

Extra credit: get involved with one somehow.

Make up your own word. Write it here with its definition:

Join an English conversation club for recent immigrants.

(1/4) Do you have a theme song? If not, it's high time you chose one.

(2/4) Start the morning by dancing to your theme song.

(3/4) Sing it out loud in the shower, bath or car.

(4/4) Keep your theme song in your head all day.

Write a letter to the editor.

Write a haiku about something you experienced today:

What one small environmental change could you make?

Read a fairy tale. Extra credit: find one from a different culture than your own.

Dine at a restaurant with communal tables.

Go to a new cafe and people-watch for an hour.

Spruce up your water today. Add cucumber and mint; grapefruit and rosemary; strawberry, basil and lemon.

Make a photo album of your town on social media.

Go to a public square and count the pigeons.

Plant something alive in a planter, milk carton, community garden or whatever else works.

Where's the most beautiful place you've ever been? Scroll through an image search until you remember exactly what it felt like to be there.

Kick, throw, bounce or somehow interact with a ball.

Sketch an image from your dream last night:

Watch street performers as if you'd bought an expensive ticket to their show.

Search for a modern art piece in a museum, cafe or online. Look at it or read about it until you get it. Or get why you don't like it.

Next time you want to cancel plans or a party because you had a long day at work? Don't.

Organise a good old-fashioned street party.

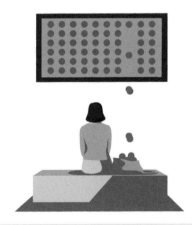

Travel really, really locally. Imagine travelling down to your toes or fingertips or up your back until you slosh around your brain.

What song have you not heard in, like, forever? Play it. Extra credit: write down the memory it evokes:

Think of a friend you haven't seen in over a month. Then buy a postcard and send it to them.

Travel internationally in your nearest city: visit three shops stocking goods from different parts of the world.

(1/2) Interested in a historical era? Find a novel based in it.

(2/2) Interested in another culture? Locate a novel written by one of its authors.

What's that one really fun thing you keep putting off because you're too busy/stressed/broke? Write down one mini-step that you could take towards doing it now:

Take the time to inspect a cloud above you. Draw it here:

Take a five-minute break at the end of each hour today. Extra credit: do something fun, adventurous or creative away from work or a computer during each break.

Out of the blue, tell someone what you appreciate about them.

Buy something sweet from a vending machine.

Play with your food today: find ways to express yourself through food art.

Make someone a gift.

Bake a loaf of bread from scratch.

Browse a second-hand bookshop and buy a book purely on the basis of its cover.

Find your pulse in your wrist or neck. Feel the sensation for one full minute. Extra credit: see if you can slow it down in the second minute.

Stay in a hotel in your home city.

Draw an outline of your hand and turn it into a piece of art:

Take a rubbing of an urban fossil. It could be a wall, a manhole cover or a paving stone.

Are you more of a tea shop, wine bar or local-pub person? Go to the most opposite next time.

Create a project from collected rocks: make a sand garden, paint an inspirational quote or word, or glue on googly eyes to make a pet rock.

What did you love to do as a kid? Pick one thing you could do today and find a toy shop, library or park – and do it.

Start a craft or DIY project.

(1/4) Go to your local grocer's shop. Pick what seems to be the 'first' row.

(2/4) Delve through the row's shelves until you find an item you've never tried. Buy it.

(3/4) Next time you're at the grocer's, go to row #2 and do the same thing.

(4/4) Then row #3, row #4 and so on until you've gone through the entire shop.

Enter a contest: photography, writing, sweepstakes to win free travel etc.

This week, buy one thing locally that you'd normally only buy online.

What emotion is the colour yellow? How about green? Silver?

Read a book by an adventurer.

In the next hour, casually fit a sentence into conversation that no one on Earth has ever said before.

You know that travel photo you love? Frame it or transfer it on to canvas so you can look at it every day.

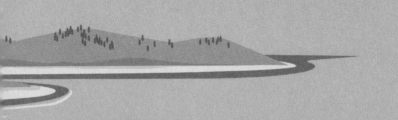

What's the closest body of water to you? Go there and ask the 55–60% of your body that's water to say hi. You're practically family, after all.

Jump on a random bus and see where it takes you.

The next time you walk somewhere, swing your arms a full 21.7% more than you normally do.

Unless absolutely necessary, don't do a single chore today.

Send a little gift to a friend. Just because.

Become a tree-hugger. Literally. Hug a tree.

Micro-libraries are popping up around the world.
Find three near you.

Give yourself a one-minute massage. Extra credit: add a scent and breathe-in deeply.

Name three things you're grateful for in your own town.

Do something you're bad at. Extra credit: do it until you go up one level.

Which organisations in your town could use your volunteer skills? Write down what you find here:

Leave your phone at home for the day.

What's your favourite TV episode of all time? Go ahead and watch it again tonight.

Write a secret note for a friend, colleague or family member and hide it somewhere for them to find in the next few days.

Walk around for an hour as if you've just received the best news ever. How does the world respond?

Take your old blankets or towels to a local animal shelter.

That weird dream you had once? Write down here
how you'd have liked it to finish:

(1/4) Ask a friend or colleague what adventurous or challenging thing they've always wished they could do.

(2/4) Ask yourself what adventurous or challenging thing you've always wished you could do.

(3/4) Make a pact with that friend or colleague to support each other in doing your adventurous or challenging thing.

(4/4) Write down the first step here:

Find the nearest purple object. What is it? Describe it.

Do you know someone who's struggling with a physical or mental health problem? Ask them if there's one thing you could do for them.

Polish something until it's shiny or clear again: a window, a shoe, a piece of jewellery or silverware.

If you told a story on stage about your life, what story would it be?

Buy a kite, bubbles or a flying disc. Go outside to play.

What smell brings back a treasured travel memory?
Suntan lotion? Incense? Fresh croissants?
Find that smell, close your eyes and let
yourself be transported.

Choose an adjective. Optimistic? Spontaneous? Naughty? (Or one of your own.) Live by that word all day.

Write a letter to someone who made a difference in your life.

(1/2) Psychologists say that asking for a favour is a great way to make a friend. Ask someone for a favour.

(2/2) Say yes to the next favour you're asked.

Teach yourself five words in your country's sign language.

Do you always go to a friend's or an appointment a few miles away by bus or car? The next time you have an hour, walk there instead.

Conduct an informational interview. Find someone willing who's in a profession that intrigues you and bring them coffee or lunch, or ask to follow them at work for a day.

Today, note how many times you laugh or smile. Extra credit: aim to top that number by one tomorrow.

Learn a new card game by playing it with a friend.

Watch a foreign film.

Extra credit: make a dish to go with it.

Read a book by a local author.

Safaris can happen anywhere. Find endemic species (plants and animals native to your region only) and go on a photography adventure.

Take a blanket to the park. Sit and read for an hour.

Shop at the nearest farmers' market you've never visited.

With no destination in mind for the first five minutes, start to drive or board a bus.

Look up the words to a song you like. Extra credit: memorise them.

Browse in a charity shop or antiques store.

Create a gift list. The next time a friend or a family member mentions a hobby they'd like to try or something they've always wanted, add it to the list in preparation for the next birthday or holiday.

Analyse your dream last night. What was in it that you'd like to know more about?

Pretend that a camera crew is following you around today.

When you see someone being grumpy or mean, imagine they're going through the worst year of their life.

Stand up as straight as possible all day. How did it change your interactions?

Pet a dog.

In 150 words, describe your civilisation – whatever that means to you – to aliens from another planet:

Invite the 'new kid'
(at work, in town,
in your country)
out for lunch.

Schedule an hour-long talk with someone who holds opposite views.

Find a nondescript street you've never been to, drive or bus there and take a walk around.

(1/4) Where is the best place that you've ever visited?

(2/4) Which food reminds you of that place? Search for it near where you live.

(3/4) What music or art reminds you of that place? Play the music or view the art.

(4/4) When you think of this trip, the first feeling or word that comes to mind is _____. Where or how can you recreate that feeling in your own town?

Go to a restaurant you've never been to before and ask the waiter to order for you.

Plan a hotel getaway in your own town. Check into a local hotel, get room service and hang out in the pool or hot tub.

What's your favourite texture? Brick? Mountains? Polka dots? Where can you find it near you?

Visit a garden centre
and browse until you
discover one new thing.

Pick one vitamin, then research which foods contain large amounts of it. What recipe can you make with those ingredients?

Which restaurant in your town has been around for the longest? Go!

Spend the day somewhere beautiful and don't take a single photograph.

Attend the next cultural festival held in your town.

Dance in a culture not your own.

Go line dancing; take a West African dance class;
shake your hips to samba.

Listen to music from a different culture for the entire day.

In your stand-up comedy routine, what three life observations would you make?

For the last minute of your shower or bath, adjust the water temperature to as cold as you can possibly stand it.

In a search engine, type one of your hobbies + a place you're planning to visit one day (ie, Scrabble + Bangkok, photography + Addis Ababa). Find a club, meeting or online group in that place and make friends who you can meet in person one day.

Undertake a science project.

Come up with your own prompt.

(Leap prompt) Open a blank document. Title it 'My Book'. Write one sentence. Congratulations, you're writing a book!

Explore Every Day

November 2019
Published by Lonely Planet Global Limited
CRN 554153
www.lonelyplanet.com
10 9 8 7 6 5 4 3 2 1
Printed in Malaysia
ISBN 9781788686358
© Lonely Planet 2019

Managing Director, Publishing Piers Pickard
Associate Publisher Robin Barton
Art Director Daniel Di Paolo
Design & Layout Tina García
Illustrator Bea Crespo
Writer Alex Leviton
Editor Nick Mee
Print Production Nigel Longuet

About the author: Lonely Planet author, sometimes start-up director and creative coach Alex Leviton has been advocating for more creativity, exploration, and play for almost 20 years. Since getting a master's in journalism from UC Berkeley, she's contributed to dozens of Lonely Planet titles, done stand-up comedy, mentored teen poets, led travel writing workshops around the world, and performed Improv badly. However, her favourite thing is to help others find their creative voice. Find her at www.alexleviton.com.

STAY IN TOUCH lonelyplanet.com/contact

Australia
The Malt Store, Level 3,
551 Swanston St, Carlton, Victoria 3053
T: 03 8379 8000

USA
124 Linden St, Oakland,
CA 94607
T: 510 250 6400

Ireland
Digital Depot, Roe Lane (off Thomas St),
Digital Hub, Dublin 8 D08 TCV4

Europe
240 Blackfriars Rd,
London SE1 8NW
T: 020 3771 5100